A Perspectives Flip Book

The Split History of the

ENGLISH CIVIL WAR

THE ROYALIST PERSPECTIVE

BY CLAIRE THROP

CONTENT CONSULTANT:
Dr Linsey Hunter
Lecturer and Teaching Assistant at the University of the Highlands and Islands

raintree
a Capstone company — publishers for children

Raintree is an imprint of Capstone Global Library Limited, a company incorporated in England
and Wales having its registered office at 264 Banbury Road, Oxford, OX2 7DY – Registered
company number: 6695582

www.raintree.co.uk
myorders@raintree.co.uk

Edited by Helen Cox Cannons
Designed by Philippa Jenkins
Original illustrations © Capstone Global Library Ltd 2016
Picture research by Kelly Garvin
Production by Victoria Fitzgerald
Originated by Capstone Global Library Ltd
Printed and bound in China

ISBN 978 1 4747 2671 9
20 19 18 17 16
10 9 8 7 6 5 4 3 2 1

ACKNOWLEDGEMENTS

We would like to thank the following for permission to reproduce photographs:
Royalist Perspective: Alamy/De Luan, 27; Bridgeman Images: The Battle of Preston and Walton,
August 17th, 1648, 1877 (w/c on paper), Cattermole, Charles (1832-1900) / Harris Museum and Art
Gallery, Preston, Lancashire, UK, 23; Mary Evan Picture Library, cover (bottom); Newscom: akg-
images, 25, akg-images/Rabatti-Domingie, 6, Design Pics, 9, 13, 16, World History Archive, 14, 21;
Oxford Designers and Illustrators, 11, 18; Superstock/Pantheon/Pantheon, cover (top).
Parliamentarian Perspective: Alamy: GL Archive, 28, Mary Evans Picture Library, 7, 19,
Sueddeutsche Zeitung Photo, 27, Timewatch Images, 12; Mary Evans Picture Library, cover (top);
GROSVENOR PRINTS, 23; Newscom: Design Pics, 9, World History Archive, 5, 21; Oxford
Designers and Illustrators, 14; Superstock/Pantheon/Pantheon, cover (bottom); The Image Works/
Topham, 17.

We would like to thank Dr Linsey Hunter for her invaluable help in the preparation of this book.

Every effort has been made to contact copyright holders of material reproduced in this book. Any
omissions will be rectified in subsequent printings if notice is given to the publisher.

Contents

SHARED RESOURCES

CHAPTER 1

CHARLES'S PERSONAL RULE

*C*harles I became king in 1625. After four years of problems with Parliament – the body of men responsible for, among other things, raising money for the king through taxes – Charles decided to dissolve (dismiss) Parliament. He did not call another Parliament until 1640. This period is known as Charles's Personal Rule, or the "Eleven Years' Tyranny" by his enemies.

Charles inherited no money in the royal coffers, so he had to find ways to both save and raise money himself during his reign. England was at war with France and Spain, so Charles made peace with both countries to save money. He also increased fines, taxes and trade with other countries.

One of the most hated taxes was ship money, a yearly tax for maintaining the navy. It was originally a tax on coastal towns to pay for the navy in emergencies, but from 1635, Charles extended it to inland towns and in times of peace. He thought it would be fairer for everyone to contribute, not just those living near the sea. However, people became increasingly annoyed with it – it was like a new tax because Parliament had never approved it. One Member of

Parliament (MP), John Hampden, was even sent to prison after refusing to pay the tax in 1637.

Charles increased his own income from £600,000 to £900,000 per year during Personal Rule. People were beginning to think Charles would never call Parliament again.

```
CHARLES 1

Charles was short, stubborn, had a stammer and
was lacking in confidence. He often assumed
people would do as he said because he was the
king. This was not the case in a time when
people expected the king to work with Parliament.
Charles found it difficult to communicate with
others, partly because of his stammer, and he
often chose to listen to the wrong people when
making important decisions.
```

THE DIVINE RIGHT OF KINGS

Charles believed in the Divine Right of kings. This meant that he thought that God gave kings the right to rule, which meant kings did not have to answer to anyone else on Earth. This belief led Charles to dislike Parliament because its members wanted him to listen to grievances (complaints) before they would give him money. Parliament was supposed to allow fairer representation for ordinary people, so Charles's ruling without its involvement was deeply unpopular.

RELIGION

There were also reforms, or changes, made to the Church, which many suspected were introduced by Charles for his Catholic wife, Henrietta Maria.

English Protestantism at the time was based on the teachings of John Calvin, a leader in the Reformation (the period when the Christian Church split into Catholicism and Protestantism). King Charles didn't trust either Calvinism or a more extreme version of Protestantism called Puritanism. However, his attempts to bring in a High Church form of religion (see box) led to people thinking "popery", or a return to Catholicism, was coming next.

Charles I and Henrietta Maria

HIGH CHURCH

Charles was an Anglican Protestant, but many believed he was Catholic because he followed a form of religion known as High Church. It fell somewhere between Protestantism and Catholicism. High Church followers agreed with Catholics that the priest was a middleman between God and people. They liked the Catholic Church ceremony, which was not appreciated by Protestants, particularly the Puritans. The High Church emphasized royal authority, which Protestants also disliked.

CHARLES AND LAUD

The Archbishop of Canterbury, William Laud, was one of the king's favourites. He gradually became more involved in matters of state, which annoyed many people who believed that Church and state should be separate. Laud tried to make all churches use the ceremonies that Laud – and the king – favoured. He made use of church courts, such as the Star Chamber and High Commission, to punish those who did not obey the rules or who complained about them. One of the best-known cases was that of Puritans William Prynne, Henry Burton and John Bastwick in 1637. They wrote pamphlets to make people aware of the religious policies of Archbishop Laud. The men were tortured and imprisoned for speaking out.

CHAPTER 2

SCOTTISH REBELLION

*I*n 1637, Charles and Archbishop Laud demanded that Scotland use the Church of England prayer book and follow the English Church. Charles was not worried about the effects of introducing the Book of Common Prayer to Scotland. He thought it would bring the two kingdoms together so he did it, but without asking either members of the Church of Scotland or the general public beforehand. Charles was out of touch with his people and their beliefs.

This resulted in a riot in St Giles Cathedral, Edinburgh. Protests spread across the country. Opponents signed an agreement called the Scottish National Covenant that called for a rejection of Charles's reforms. These opponents became known as Covenanters.

THE COVENANTERS

The Covenanters were Scottish Presbyterians who signed the National Covenant in February 1638. Scottish nobles also joined the protesters because they were unhappy about Charles's attempts to weaken their power. Many ordinary people supported the Covenanters and they soon became the main religious and political power in Scotland.

The Covenanters protested against the attempts by Charles I and William Laud (pictured, standing) to force changes in the Scottish Church.

THE FIRST BISHOPS' WAR

Charles was unwilling to compromise with the Covenanters, so he marched to Scotland with an army in 1639. The Covenanters formed their own, very religious army. The English army was in poor condition and lacking in experience. A truce at Berwick was the result. This lost Charles supporters in England, as they resented being asked to pay for his war, one in which he was trying to enforce a form of religion that was already disliked in England.

A NEW FAVOURITE

Thomas Wentworth, an MP and Charles's adviser, had been ruling in Ireland since 1633. He had control of the Irish Parliament, so when Charles called him back to England in 1639, and made him Earl of Strafford, he suggested the king finally call the English Parliament. Archbishop Laud backed this decision.

THE SHORT PARLIAMENT

The Short Parliament was called for about three weeks in April 1640. Charles hoped that the MPs would have forgotten the problems of the last Parliament and would vote for him to have the money for his army straight away. They hadn't forgotten – they wanted their grievances heard before they would consider taxation.

John Pym, one of the leading MPs, called for consideration of the rights of Parliament. He suggested that the House of Lords join the Commons and Charles to try to solve the problems. Charles disliked Pym and found it difficult to work with him. Charles dissolved Parliament again. The Earl of Northumberland, one of Charles's supporters involved in battles against the Covenanters, wrote to Viscount Conway in May 1640: "I think they [Parliament] might in time have got what they wanted. But they went on with their business in a noisy and confused way, which offended His Majesty so much that this morning he ended the Parliament."

THE COVENANTERS WIN AGAIN

In August 1640, the Covenanters, led by General Leslie, once again beat Charles, this time at the Battle of Newburn. Covenanters came as far south as Newcastle and would not leave. The English army under Strafford was forced to retreat to Durham.

The Covenanters now had control of the coal supply, so Charles had no option but to negotiate the Treaty of London. Part of the terms of the Treaty of London was that Charles had to pay the Covenanters a large sum of money. Charles was forced to call

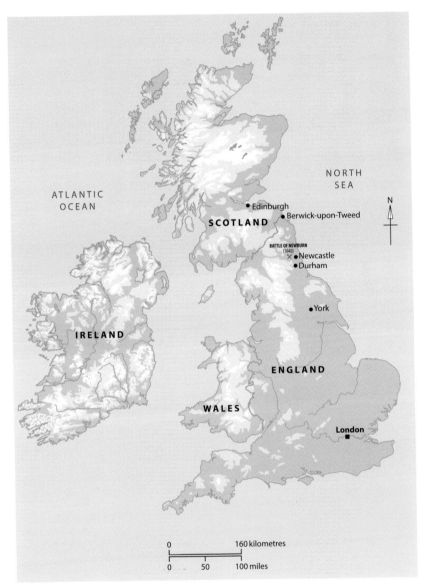

This map shows where the Battle of Newburn took place.

Parliament again in November of that year, as he did not have the money to pay the Covenanters. He hoped that this time Parliament would be more willing to help. Also, Parliament had to approve the Treaty of London, which was finally signed in August 1641.

CHAPTER 3

THE LONG PARLIAMENT

Before they would help the king, members of the Long Parliament stated their disapproval of his war with Scotland. They then set about reversing the methods used during Charles's Personal Rule, such as the outdated forms of taxation and his use of church courts. The king was isolated – his ministers had fled or been arrested. He had little choice but to agree to suggestions, including the banning of ship money, the calling of Parliament every three years (the Triennial Act) and that Parliament could not be dismissed without the permission of its own members.

IMPEACHMENT

In the 17th century, impeachment was a way for Parliament to get rid of unpopular ministers, particularly favourites of the king or queen. Ministers could be impeached for treason (betraying a person's own country). Members of the House of Commons would argue the crimes of the person on trial and the House of Lords would act as the judge.

A. Doctor Vsher Lord Primate of Ireland,
B the Sherifes of London,
C the Earle of Strafford
D his kindred and friends.

Charles felt guilty about Strafford's execution for the rest of his life.

STRAFFORD'S EXECUTION

While in Ireland, Strafford had raised an army to control the country, but had not treated Catholics badly afterwards. To Parliament, this meant he must be a supporter of Catholicism. Charles had promised Strafford he would never let him be harmed, but when Strafford reached London in order to impeach the leaders of the Commons for treason, Pym impeached him first.

Strafford was put on trial for high treason in March 1641, accused of offering Charles the (Catholic) Irish army to fight the Covenanters. Strafford defended himself well. Pym then called for a Bill of Attainder, which would make him guilty without a trial – this would, in effect, result in a death sentence. Both the Commons and the Lords passed it. King Charles sent his son, also Charles, to persuade Parliament to make his punishment life imprisonment instead. Eventually, Strafford wrote to the king, realizing that his death was the only chance of saving England from civil war. Strafford was executed on 12 May 1641.

PARLIAMENT SPLIT

By late 1641, Parliament was no longer united against the king. The Grand Remonstrance listed Parliament's 204 grievances against the king, which included taxation, land confiscation and foreign policy. It only narrowly passed in the Commons and was hardly supported in the Lords. MPs also tried to get control of the army – they feared that Charles would use the army fighting the Ulster Rebellion in Ireland against them. However, the king refused to give up command.

Gradually, the king gained more supporters, especially religious traditionalists. He felt the tide had turned, so he decided to arrest the five leaders who had been his strongest opponents, including Pym and

On 4 January 1642, Charles entered the House of Commons with armed guards to arrest five MPs, but they had been warned and had escaped.

Hampden. This was controversial because the king could not enter Parliament without being invited. This was so that MPs felt able to speak freely.

HULL

Charles set up court in York while his queen, Henrietta Maria, went to Europe to get support and money by selling some crown jewels. When Charles tried to gather weapons from those left at the Hull garrison after the Bishops' Wars, Sir John Hotham refused him entry. Royalists put the city under siege, but gunfire drove them away.

GATHERING SUPPORT

In March, Parliament pushed through the Militia Ordinance, which forced each county's militia (soldiers) to be under Parliament's control. The king issued commissions of array (an ancient method of raising troops) to encourage counties to raise troops for him, not Parliament. Counties now had to choose sides. Some, including the people of Somerset, who wrote to Charles, were unhappy: "We humbly ask to avoid the miseries that may befall us by means of contrary [different] commands…"

NINETEEN PROPOSITIONS

Parliament sent the king the Nineteen Propositions in June. Parliament wanted a larger share of power, so they demanded, among other things, control of the army and the ability to choose the king's ministers. Charles rejected the demands. War was now unavoidable.

CHAPTER 4

THE FIRST CIVIL WAR

Charles declared war on Parliament at Nottingham on 22 August 1642. He'd chosen Nottingham because he hoped to get support from the country of Holland, which would require access via the River Trent.

EDGEHILL

The first major battle of the Civil War was at Edgehill in October. The Royalist cavalry, led by Charles's nephew Prince Rupert,

Charles I (left, waving) hoped people would rally to him at Nottingham, due to its central location.

beat the Parliamentarian cavalry. There were many inexperienced soldiers on both sides and the Royalists were trying out a new, Swedish-style troop formation. In the end, the Royalists made a mistake in pursuing the Parliamentarians too far from the field, which prevented a decisive win.

ROYALIST VICTORIES

Further Royalist wins came in late 1642 and early 1643. But at Turnham Green in November, Parliament's army prevented Charles's marching to London. The Royalists retreated to Oxford. This city remained the Royalists' base for the rest of the war.

July 1643 saw the Royalists take Bristol by force. This was an important win as they now had control of a port. Bristol factories also produced more muskets (guns) for the army.

HELP NEEDED

Parliament knew they were losing, so they sought help from the Scottish Covenanters, signing the Solemn League and Covenant in September 1643. They had to agree to reform the English Church to match the Scottish one.

Charles had hoped for help from Europe, but it never came. Instead, he organized a truce in Ireland – the Cessation – so that about 10,000 government soldiers could fight for him in England. Parliament used this to scare English Protestants, suggesting Charles was siding with Catholics.

BATTLE OF MARSTON MOOR

The tide began to turn with the Battle of Marston Moor on 2 July 1644. Oliver Cromwell's cavalry destroyed the Royalist's cavalry – the first time this had happened. Cromwell was an MP who had worked his way up the army ranks during the war. His cavalry was well trained and disciplined. The Covenanter army also helped defeat Charles. Charles had now virtually lost the north of England, his biggest support base.

NEW MODEL ARMY

The New Model Army Ordinance of February 1645 created a professional national army. Cromwell set it up, having been unhappy with the way the war had been fought so far. Most Royalists were not impressed – the New Model Army was inexperienced in actual warfare. Prince Rupert thought the ideals were good, but he failed in his attempt to instil some of them into his own Royalist soldiers.

This map shows where the Battles of Edgehill, Marston Moor and Naseby took place.

BATTLE OF NASEBY

Charles's army had besieged Leicester successfully in May 1645, so he perhaps had an exaggerated idea of how strong his army was when he marched to relieve Oxford, which was being besieged by the New Model Army. Other Royalists, including Prince Rupert, had recommended going north. Fairfax, leader of the New Model Army, marched to meet Charles, but both had to wait for their support to arrive before fighting. Fairfax's support – Cromwell – was nearer. The king's support didn't reach him in time. The Royalists were outnumbered but more experienced.

The Battle of Naseby was in the balance until Cromwell entered the action. He was an able leader, and some Royalist survivors said they thought Cromwell's cavalry, known as the Ironsides, made the difference. The Royalists had underestimated the New Model Army, which had been trained well. Out of about 12,500 royalists, fewer than 4,000 made it to safety, and some of those were severely wounded.

SURRENDER

The last Royalist army was defeated at Stow-on-the-Wold in March 1646. The New Model Army besieged Oxford from 3 May. The Covenanters had been working for Parliament, but Charles now decided his best move was to play them against Parliament. Charles surrendered to the Covenanters, who were camped at Newark, on 6 May 1646. Oxford, where Charles had based his court, surrendered to Parliament on 24 June.

CHAPTER 5

NEGOTIATIONS AND WAR

After Charles surrendered, it took months to negotiate a settlement that pleased the king, the New Model Army and Parliament. The Covenanters had moved Charles to Newcastle, a more easily defendable location. In July 1646, the king was presented with the Newcastle Propositions (which were the Nineteen Propositions plus the 1643 Treaty with the Covenanters). The king had no intention of signing, but he delayed because he knew that the relationship between the Covenanters and Parliament was strained. At the same time, he was secretly negotiating with Ireland and France. In January 1647, Parliament told the Covenanters that they were no longer needed. Parliament's actions helped Charles by causing some Scots to change sides. Men like the Duke of Hamilton believed Charles as king would keep the peace in Scotland.

Parliament also disbanded the New Model Army. Cromwell thought the English soldiers were treated badly, so he left London on 4 June 1647 to join up with the New Model Army.

THE ARMY STAKES ITS CLAIM

On the same day, a New Model Army officer and 500 men seized Charles. Cromwell and his son-in-law, Henry Ireton, negotiated with Charles at Newmarket. Cromwell tried to assure the army that they could trust Charles and Parliament, but they could not reach an agreement despite the generous terms. The king was moved to Hampton Court in August. However, he escaped in November and went to Carisbrooke Castle on the Isle of Wight. From there, he negotiated with the Scots and Irish.

AGREEMENT WITH THE SCOTS

The Scots were now divided: the Duke of Argyll headed the Covenanters sympathetic to Parliament, while the Duke of Hamilton and his brother led another group more sympathetic to the king.

The Covenanters handed King Charles I (seated) over to Parliament. He was imprisoned at Holdenby House in Northamptonshire.

They became known as the Engagers after the Engagement, or agreement, they arranged with Charles in December 1647.

Charles would have to take the Oath of Covenant to bring the English Church in line with the Scottish Church. Many Royalists thought this cost too high, but Charles agreed to it. It is doubtful that he ever intended to keep this promise. He was happy to join whichever side was likely to help him regain his throne.

SECOND CIVIL WAR

By January 1648, the Scots' Engagement and the growing divide between the army and Parliament inspired the Royalists, so they set war in motion again. From April to September, rebellions against Parliament broke out in England, Wales and Scotland.

Cromwell and the army defeated an uprising in Wales and then crushed the undisciplined Scottish Engager Army and northern Royalists at the Battle of Preston in August 1648.

CHARLES NEGOTIATES

After the Royalists' defeat, Charles negotiated with the traditionalists in Parliament in September 1648, which led to the Treaty of Newport. The Puritans in Parliament, and the army, were unhappy. They felt Charles had gone too far in encouraging the Second Civil War. The king had been shown to be untrustworthy, negotiating with all sides.

The Battle of Preston was fought over two days during August 1648. Fighting was fierce and bloody. The defeat of the Royalist and Scottish Engager Army forces left Charles with no decent power base in England.

ARMY DEMANDS

The army now felt that all negotiations with the king should be stopped. In the Army Remonstrance of November 1648, it was suggested that Charles be put on trial as an enemy of his people. But army commanders rejected the Remonstrance. It was only when they heard that the king was to come to London to complete the treaty that they decided to do something drastic. Henry Ireton suggested that the army purge (rid) Parliament of all MPs who were negotiating with Charles. This led to Pride's Purge on 6 December. The 80 MPs who were left became known as the Rump Parliament.

The Rump created the High Court of Justice to put the king on trial. John Bradshaw, a local judge known to be anti-Royalist, agreed to lead the trial.

CHAPTER 6
DEATH OF A KING

Charles's trial took place at Westminster Hall on 20 January 1649. The High Court of Justice had 135 members but not all attended: for example Fairfax and Oliver St John did not. Some people worried that there would be an attempt to rescue the king, so security was fierce: the cellars and roofs were checked and guards watched the court at all times.

Parliament had the problem of what charge they could bring against the king. In the end, they invented a new definition of treason: "It is treason in the King of England… to levy [make] war against the Parliament and Kingdom of England".

Charles appeared in the court four times, but he continued to say that he believed the court to be unlawful. As Charles believed that kings were appointed by God, he also believed that he was above the power of the courts to try him. Charles stated, "A king cannot be tried by any superior jurisdiction [power] on Earth". Also, Pride's Purge meant that the full Parliament wasn't even there – how could they be representative of the people? Charles refused to plead guilty or not guilty, but stated that he stood "for the liberty [freedom] of the people of England".

On 27 January, after refusing the king permission to give a speech in his own defence, Bradshaw declared Charles guilty. The king would be beheaded. He was removed from the court while still complaining about being silenced. Fewer than half of the members of the court signed the death warrant.

EXECUTION OF THE KING

Charles was beheaded outside the Banqueting Hall at Whitehall on 30 January 1649. He wore two shirts so that the people watching would not think he was shivering with fear.

The crowd groaned when the axe chopped off their king's head.

CROMWELL

A 41-member Council of State was set up to run the country alongside the House of Commons (the Rump) after Charles's death. The Rump Parliament announced that the House of Lords and the monarchy were no more.

THE THIRD CIVIL WAR

Charles, eldest son of Charles I, took up the fight for the throne after his father's death. His original plan was to use Ireland as a base, but Cromwell's actions meant he needed to rethink.

IRELAND

Cromwell made many enemies in Ireland after he was sent to establish control there in August 1649. The Royalist town of Drogheda was well defended, but even so it was unable to withstand the bombardment and massacre of 11 September. A further massacre at Wexford a few weeks later meant that control in Ireland was gained quickly. Cromwell's success in Ireland was also partly due to a potato famine there that was causing mass starvation. By May 1650, Cromwell was able to return to England.

While on the run, Charles famously hid in Boscobel oak tree.

SCOTLAND

Charles arrived in Scotland from Europe in June 1650. Cromwell and the New Model Army were sent to Scotland to prevent an invasion of England. Against the odds, the Scottish Royalists were heavily beaten at Dunbar in September. Not only did they outnumber the Parliamentarians, but the day before battle they were camped on high ground. Strangely, they decided to move down the hill onto level ground to fight. Until then, Cromwell's only option seemed to be escape by sea.

BATTLE OF WORCESTER

On 1 January 1651 at Scone, the Scots crowned Charles II King of Scotland. He and the Scots then marched into England. Charles attracted few recruits in England and some Scots deserted once the army passed Carlisle. The Royalists met the Parliamentarians at the Battle of Worcester on 3 September.

Despite Charles's bravery – "Certainly a braver prince never lived", wrote one Royalist – they were heavily outnumbered and lost the battle. Worcester was the last battle of the Civil Wars. Charles had to escape. He was on the run for six weeks before sailing to France in October.

PROBLEMS WITH PARLIAMENT

After the Third Civil War, Cromwell thought Parliament would now be free to push through religious changes, but they were reluctant. They were also worried about the growing power of the army. Cromwell finally dismissed the Rump Parliament in April 1653.

The Barebones Parliament sat from July 1653. It was made up of "godly" (religious) men chosen by Cromwell. However, many were too keen on reform, which Cromwell realized would further alienate the people. After the MPs argued between themselves, most decided to resign (leave). The army removed the others.

LORD PROTECTOR

In December 1653, a group of army officers wrote a new constitution called the Instrument of Government, which allowed Cromwell to become Lord Protector of the Commonwealth. Cromwell was later offered the throne, but refused it.

More problems between Cromwell and Parliament followed, so in 1655, a new system was tried out: regional rule by the army's Major-Generals. These men were powerful and they trained new militia funded by a tax on Royalists. Puritans became powerful, which led to changes in churches – they were much plainer than before. Certain activities such as dancing and going to the theatre were banned.

THE RESTORATION

Oliver Cromwell died in 1658, leaving his son Richard to take over the Protectorship. The army was owed pay, and some thought that Richard was a bad choice for Lord Protector. Richard calmed the situation for a while, but he was a weak leader. Tension soon erupted again.

RETURN OF THE RUMP

George Monck, who had been a general under Oliver Cromwell, realized that something had to be done to prevent another civil war. Monck and the army marched to London in January 1660, and brought back the MPs who had been purged from the Rump Parliament in 1648. Parliament agreed that an elected Parliament and a king would be best for the country.

KING AND PARLIAMENT

In April, in the Declaration of Breda, Charles II stated that he would do his best to solve problems, such as paying the army and pardoning those who had acted against his father. In May, a newly elected Parliament voted to restore the monarchy. Charles returned to England to a joyful welcome. This time, however, Parliament made sure that power was shared more evenly between king and Parliament. In April 1661, Charles II was crowned at Westminster.

INDEX

GLOSSARY

ALLEGIANCE — loyalty to a particular person or cause

BESIEGE — surround a place or building with armed soldiers in order to force the people inside to surrender

CATHOLIC — Christian who is a member of the Roman Catholic Church, led by the Pope

COMMONWEALTH — country that is not governed by a king or queen but by a representative of the people

CONSTITUTION — document that sets out how a country is to be governed

DISSOLVE — dismiss

GRIEVANCE — complaint

HOUSE OF COMMONS — part of Parliament that includes people elected as MPs

HOUSE OF LORDS — part of Parliament that includes nobles and bishops

IMPEACHMENT — charge of a crime against a person's own country

MILITIA — armed force raised from ordinary people, not professional soldiers

MP — Member of Parliament

PROTECTORATE — time during which a Protector, or chosen leader, rules a country or state

PROTESTANT — member of any of the Christian churches that broke away from the Roman Catholic Church during the 1500s

RADICAL — extreme

REFORM — change something

REFORMATION — religious change in which Protestant churches were set up in opposition to the teachings of the Roman Catholic Church

TAX — money paid to the government on certain items or income

TRAITOR — person who has betrayed his or her own country

TREASON — betraying or committing a crime against your own country, monarch or government

TRUCE — agreement between sides in a war to stop fighting for a certain period of time

TYRANNY — cruel, harsh style of government

TIMELINE

1625
Charles I becomes king

1629-1640
Eleven Years' Tyranny or Charles I's Personal Rule

1639/1640
Bishops' Wars

1641
Ulster Rebellion

Aug: The Treaty of London is signed

Nov: Grand Remonstrance passes through Parliament

1642
4 Jan: Charles enters House of Commons in an attempt to arrest five MPs on charges of high treason

22 Aug: Charles raises standard at Nottingham (start of First Civil War)

23 Oct: Battle of Edgehill

1648
17-19 Aug: Battle of Preston (start of Second Civil War)

Nov: Army Remonstrance

6 Dec: Pride's Purge

1649
20-27 Jan: Charles I's trial

May: England declared a Commonwealth

11 Sep: Battle of Drogheda, Ireland

1650
3 Sep: Battle of Dunbar, Scotland

1651
3 Sep: Battle of Worcester, England (end of Civil Wars)

1643

25 Sep: Signing of Solemn League and Covenant between Parliament and the Scots

1644

2 July: Battle of Marston Moor

1645

17 Feb: New Model Army Ordinance

14 June: Battle of Naseby (end of First Civil War)

1646

May: Charles surrenders to the Scots

1647

Jan: Charles handed over to Parliament

4 June: New Model Army captures Charles

11 Nov: Charles escapes to Isle of Wight

1653

Apr: Long Parliament finally dismissed

July–Dec: Barebones Parliament

Dec: Cromwell becomes Lord Protector

1658

Sep: Cromwell dies; Richard Cromwell, his son, becomes Lord Protector

1661

Apr: Charles II is crowned king (The Restoration)

SELECT BIBLIOGRAPHY

A History of Britain, Volume 2: The British Wars 1603–1776, Simon Schama (BBC Worldwide, 2001)

Battlefield Britain, Peter and Dan Snow (BBC Books, 2004)

Civil War, Taylor Downing and Maggie Millman (Parkgate Books, 1998)

Cromwell: Our Chief of Men, Antonia Fraser (Phoenix, 1973; 2002 ed.)

King Charles II, Antonia Fraser (Phoenix, 1979; 2002 ed.)

National Archives: **www.nationalarchives.gov.uk/education/civilwar/**

The English Civil Wars, Blair Worden (Phoenix, 2009)

PLACES TO VISIT

Houses of Parliament
Westminster
London SW1A 0AA

www.parliament.uk/visiting
You can visit the Houses of Parliament and take a tour around these famous buildings.

Oliver Cromwell's House
29 St Mary's Street
Ely
Cambridgeshire CB7 4HF

visitely.eastcambs.gov.uk/cromwell/oliver-cromwells-house
Oliver Cromwell and his family moved to this house in Ely in 1636. You can take a guided tour to see how the Cromwell family would have lived.

The Split History of the

ENGLISH CIVIL WAR

THE PARLIAMENTARIAN PERSPECTIVE

BY CLAIRE THROP

CONTENT CONSULTANT

Dr Linsey Hunter
Lecturer and Teaching Assistant at the University of the
Highlands and Islands

 raintree

a Capstone company — publishers for children

ABOUT THE AUTHOR:

Claire Throp grew up in High Wycombe, Buckinghamshire. She worked as an editor in publishing for 18 years before becoming an author. Claire has written books on all sorts of subjects, including history, science and geography, and now lives in Lincolnshire.

SOURCE NOTES:

Royalists' perspective
Page 9, line 7: *The English Civil Wars*, Blair Worden (Phoenix, 2009), page 28

Page 10, line 15: www.nationalarchives.gov.uk/education/civilwar/g3/cs2/s2/

Page 13, line 2: www.nationalarchives.gov.uk/education/civilwar/g3/cs2/s4/

Page 13, line 8: www.britannica.com/biography/Thomas-Wentworth-1st-Earl-of-Strafford

Page 13, line 13 *(p.32)*; page 21, line 6 *(p.67)*: *King Charles II*, Antonia Fraser (Phoenix, 1979; 2002 ed.)

Page 15, line 16: www.nationalarchives.gov.uk/education/civilwar/g3/cs2/s9/

Page 19, line 15: *Battlefield Britain*, Peter and Dan Snow (BBC Books, 2004), page 137

Page 20, line 9: http://bcw-project.org/church-and-state/second-civil-war/newcastle-propositions

Page 21, line 2; page 25, line 14: www.britannica.com/biography/Charles-I-king-of-Great-Britain-and-Ireland

Page 25, line 17: *Civil War*, Taylor Downing and Maggie Millman (Parkgate Books, 1998), page 134

Parliamentarians' perspective
Pages 6, line 3 *(p.73)*; page 23, line 9 *(p.422)*: *Cromwell: Our chief of men*, Antonia Fraser (Phoenix, 1973; 2002 ed.), page 75

Page 12, line 5 *(p.57)*; page 19, line 3 *(p.99)*: Worden

Page 19, line 3 *(p.128)*; page 21, line 6 *(p.133)*; page 22, line 2 *(p.158)*; page 24, line 12 *(p.141)*; page 26, line 6 *(p.140)*: Downing and Millman

Page 21, caption, line 1: www.parliament.uk/about/living-heritage/evolutionofparliament/parliamentaryauthority/civilwar/overview/prides-purge/

Page 23, line 5: www.bbc.co.uk/history/british/plantation/planters/es10.shtml

Page 24, line 13 *(p.133)*; page 25, line 3 *(p.140)*; page 25, line 16 *(pp. 141–142)*: *King Charles II*, Fraser

Contents

ELEVEN YEARS' TYRANNY

CHAPTER 1

ince the 14th century, Parliament in England had been divided into the House of Lords and the House of Commons. During King Charles I's reign, the Lords was full of noblemen and bishops while the House of Commons had men chosen to represent the people in their county. Parliament voted on taxes, suggested laws and advised the monarch. The king or queen had the power to call Parliament into session, and also to dissolve, or end, Parliament. Charles I dissolved Parliament three times in four years. Then, in 1629, he declared he would rule entirely without Parliament. There was a growing belief during the period that became known as Charles's Eleven Years' Tyranny that the king would never call Parliament again. Many feared that he would become an absolute monarch, as in France and Spain, where monarchs ruled without a parliament.

OPPOSITION TO THE KING

Member of Parliament (MP) John Pym was one of the first to oppose Charles. Then another MP, John Hampden, challenged Charles by refusing to pay an unpopular ship tax that he had introduced. Hampden lost the court case (7–5). Charles dismissed several of the judges who voted against him.

BISHOPS' WARS

William Laud, Archbishop of Canterbury, followed the High Church style of worship, which many people thought was too much like Catholicism. In 1637, Charles and Archbishop Laud announced that Scotland must use the Church of England prayer book and follow the High Church form of worship. After a riot in St Giles Cathedral, in Edinburgh, protests erupted all over the country. A group of people signed the Scottish National Covenant, which was an agreement that called for a rejection of the Church reforms Charles demanded. These people became known as Covenanters.

Charles went to war with the Covenanters, but was unsuccessful. He did not have the money to pay a professional army.

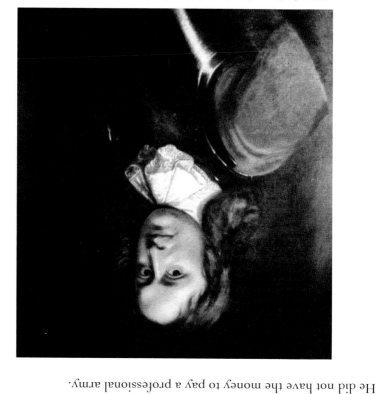

MP John Hampden claimed that the ship tax was against the Law because he didn't live in a coastal town.

PARLIAMENT
CALLED ONCE MORE

Charles's war with Scotland forced him to call Parliament in April 1640. MPs were happy to have the chance to air their grievances. First, John Pym requested an annual Parliament. Instead, Charles dismissed the Short Parliament after three weeks because they would not raise money for him.

Despite this lack of money, Charles tried to defeat the Covenanters again – with devastating results. The Earl of Strafford, one of the king's favourite ministers, led Charles's army. Strafford had successfully ruled in Ireland since 1633. The Covenanters ended up camped in Newcastle, cutting off coal supplies to southern England, and would not leave without being paid £850 a day. Charles did not have that much money, so he had to recall Parliament. This became known as the Long Parliament.

THE LONG PARLIAMENT

After the brief length of the previous Parliament, MPs were now united in opposition to the king. From 3 November 1640, leaders in the Commons, including Pym, Hampden and Oliver St John, set about overturning the issues that had emerged throughout Charles's Personal Rule, such as illegal taxation and Church court. Charles was forced to agree to the changes. He had little support after many of his ministers were arrested or forced to flee.

STRAFFORD

The House of Commons put Strafford on trial for treason. He was accused of wanting to use the Catholic Irish army to help control England. The case against him was weak and Strafford was defending himself successfully, so Pym decided that an Act of Attainder was necessary to force the death sentence. By acting this way, Pym was working outside the law in a similar way to the king. He also encouraged anti-Royalist crowds outside Westminster as debates on the act took place. The intimidation worked and the act was passed.

In May 1641, Strafford was executed.

THE GRAND REMONSTRANCE

Puritans now dominated the Commons, and they were not happy about Charles's religious and political changes. The Ulster (Irish) Rebellion had broken out in October 1641 and Parliament feared that the same army would be used against them. John Pym worried that fighting the Catholics in Ireland would make Charles stronger and more popular with the people. Pym did his best to block any attempt by Charles to go to war in Ireland. Parliament then issued the Grand Remonstrance.

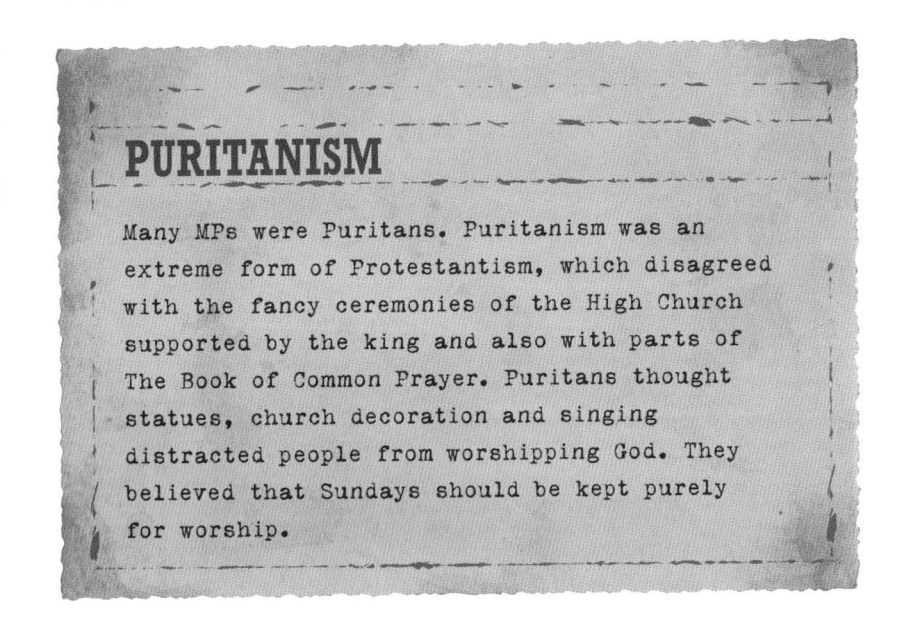

PURITANISM

Many MPs were Puritans. Puritanism was an extreme form of Protestantism, which disagreed with the fancy ceremonies of the High Church supported by the king and also with parts of The Book of Common Prayer. Puritans thought statues, church decoration and singing distracted people from worshipping God. They believed that Sundays should be kept purely for worship.

Written between August and November 1641, the Grand Remonstrance outlined all the main issues Parliament had with the king. It did not blame the king himself, but his advisers, religious or otherwise. However, it was clear that the long list of grievances referred to Charles's reign. The Remonstrance demanded that Parliament be able to approve the king's ministers.

John Pym

The Grand Remonstrance narrowly passed in the Commons on 22 November, but there was a near riot in there. It was presented to Charles on 1 December, but he ignored it. So Pym had it printed and circulated outside Parliament. Charles finally rejected it on 23 December.

PARLIAMENT SPLIT

A Royalist group (religious traditionalists) now emerged in Parliament for the first time. Parliament was no longer united against the king – there was a split between those who wanted more reforms and those who thought they'd gone far enough. The split was particularly noticeable between religious traditionalists and the Puritans.

THE FIVE MEMBERS

Charles I, feeling confident of his support, then went to the House of Commons to try to arrest the five leading opposition MPs, including Pym, and one lord, on 4 January 1642. But they had been warned and had left the building. They only returned on 11 January once the king had gone north to York. Many were outraged that Charles had entered the Commons without being invited (it was one of Parliament's rights to decide whether the monarch could enter the Commons when Parliament was in session) and had dared to try to arrest MPs. All trust between the two sides was gone.

Both sides were now readying for war. Parliament pushed through the Militia Ordinance in March, which allowed each county's militia to be under the control of a Parliament supporter. The king issued commissions of array, an ancient method of raising troops. Counties were forced to choose sides.

NINETEEN PROPOSITIONS

Parliament sent the king the Nineteen Propositions in June. They included demands for control of the army, foreign policy, the king's ministers and even the marriages of his children. There was also a section that asked for stronger anti-Catholic measures. Most MPs thought the Nineteen Propositions could be a starting point for negotiations, but the more radical MPs meant them as an ultimatum: if Charles rejected them, it meant war. Charles did indeed reject the Propositions.

CHAPTER 3
WAR BREAKS OUT

On 22 August 1642, Charles raised his standard at Nottingham, officially declaring war on Parliament.

BATTLE OF EDGEHILL

At the first major battle of the Civil War, the Battle of Edgehill, the Parliamentarian general was the Earl of Essex. His job was to prevent Charles from reaching London. The battle should have been a Royalist win, but the Royalist general, Charles's nephew Prince Rupert, took so long in pursuing the Parliamentarian cavalry (soldiers on horseback), that Parliament's infantry (soldiers on foot) were able to keep fighting and avoid a damaging loss.

CAVALIERS AND ROUNDHEADS

The names Cavaliers and Roundheads are nicknames that were given to each side by the opposition. "Cavaliers" comes from the Spanish word *caballeros*, meaning armed horsemen. Parliamentarians felt the Royalist Cavaliers were violent gentlemen. Parliamentarians were thought to be of lowly origin. They were called Roundheads because of the shaved heads of the apprentices that had been so supportive of Parliament before the war began.

SOLEMN LEAGUE AND COVENANT

By mid-1643, the Royalists had the upper hand in the war and Parliament had to act. They made an alliance with the Scots – the Solemn League and Covenant. They had to promise to preserve the Church of Scotland and reform the English Church. Parliament signed the Covenant in September. A Scottish army of about 20,000 men arrived in England in January 1644.

BATTLE OF MARSTON MOOR

On 2 July 1644, the biggest battle of the war – the Battle of Marston Moor – took place. Cromwell's cavalry (known as the Ironsides) played a big part in Parliament's win.

At the Battle of Marston Moor, in July 1644, the Royalist army was heavily outnumbered, with around 18,000 men to the Parliamentarians' 28,000 men.

OLIVER CROMWELL

Oliver Cromwell was born in Huntingdon in 1599. As a young adult, he was active in local politics and helped to fight against Charles and Archbishop Laud's religious policies. Cromwell was linked with several Puritan groups. In 1640, he was elected to the Long Parliament as an MP for Cambridge. He criticized the king's religious policies and gradually made a name for himself in political circles. After first fighting at the end of the Battle of Edgehill, he made a name for himself in military circles, too.

The Scottish army was powerful and helped to defeat the Royalists. The result was that Parliament was now in control of the north of England, which had been Charles's main area of support.

NEW MODEL ARMY

Arguments about how to conduct battles, and strange decisions made by two Parliamentarian commanders – the Earls of Essex and Manchester – led to the Royalists getting some victories in the south, even though Parliament had the upper hand overall. On 17 February 1645, Cromwell pushed through the New Model Army Ordinance. He felt the old army needed younger men, who were also professionals. Cromwell also openly criticized some of his fellow officers, including the Earl of Manchester.

The New Model Army was the first time that an army was created that allowed people to progress on their skills rather than their rank. Cromwell suggested that no MP could be commander of the army. This was the Self-Denying Ordinance and was meant to prevent unskilled men being in charge of the army. The army was now independent of Parliament.

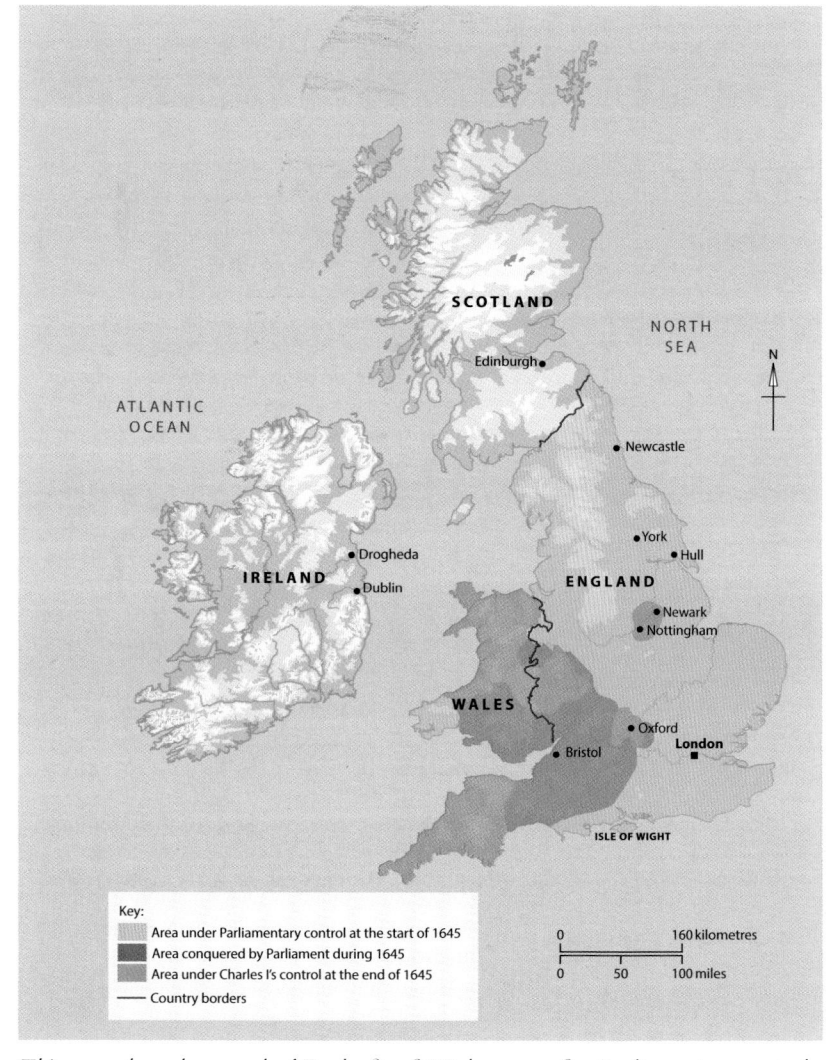

This map shows how much of England and Wales was under Parliamentary control by the end of 1645.

The New Model Army was put under the command of Sir Thomas Fairfax, who then insisted that Cromwell be second in command. The New Model Army fully supported Cromwell (many of the soldiers were Puritans, like Cromwell himself).

BATTLE OF NASEBY

The Battle of Naseby, in Northamptonshire, took place on 14 June 1645 and was decisive. The Scottish army was not involved, but Cromwell's cavalry, the Ironsides, were. Some of Charles's cavalry were in the north, so the Royalists who fought at Naseby were outnumbered.

The battle was in the balance until Cromwell entered the action. He encouraged his cavalry to attack in one mass, like a battering ram. Some Royalist survivors said they thought the Ironsides made the difference. The Royalists took a heavy beating, partly because they had underestimated the New Model Army, which had been trained well and was very disciplined.

ROYALIST SURRENDER

Within weeks, all the Royalist strongholds fell. The king had lost his best army officers and infantrymen, all his artillery and most of his weapons. In April 1646, Charles left Oxford in disguise and surrendered to the Scots at Newark. He chose the Scots rather than Parliament because the Scots still saw a monarch as part of their future government. The people of Oxford, the city that Charles had used as his base during the war, surrendered to Parliament in May.

AN UNTRUSTWORTHY KING

CHAPTER 4

In July 1646, the Newcastle Propositions were presented to Charles at Newcastle, the city to which the Covenanters had taken him. They included the Nineteen Propositions from 1642 and the 1643 Covenanter treaty. Charles once again rejected the Propositions.

After the war ended, Parliament wanted to disband the New Model Army, which angered Cromwell. He tried to bring the two together, but without success. In January 1647, Parliament also paid off the Covenanters, who then handed over the king to Parliament.

In June 1647, after Parliament hired another Scottish army to protect them from the New Model Army, Cromwell left London and joined the New Model Army. Cromwell continued to say that Parliament should be respected, but many in the army now thought that neither Parliament nor the king could be trusted.

THE ARMY TAKES THE KING

In June, George Joyce, a young New Model Army officer, and 500 soldiers, seized Charles. He was taken to the army headquarters at Newmarket. Cromwell and his son-in-law, Henry Ireton, presented Charles with a new deal, one that was better for the king than the one Parliament had offered. Charles rejected the deal.

He was moved to Hampton Court in August 1647, but in November, he escaped to the Isle of Wight. In December, Charles signed an agreement with the Scots – not with the Covenanters but with a group named the Engagers, led by the Duke of Hamilton. They named themselves the Engagers after the Engagement, or agreement, they had arranged with Charles at this time.

SECOND CIVIL WAR

The Royalists, encouraged by the fact that Cromwell had not managed to unite the army and Parliament, started the Second Civil War. A number of uprisings against Parliament broke out around the kingdom. In August 1648, Oliver Cromwell and his New Model Army finally beat the Royalists at the Battle of Preston. Cromwell had not expected to win the battle – the Royalists had more men and a better position from which to fight. He believed that the victory was a sign from God that he was on the right path.

Cromwell's forces had an unexpected win at the Battle of Preston.

After the Royalist defeat, Charles negotiated with the religious traditionalists in Parliament and in September signed the Treaty of Newport. He agreed that Parliament would have control of the militia for 20 years and that the official English religion would be Presbyterian, a form of Protestantism. However, he refused to agree to the Solemn League and Covenant, and he wanted to make sure that Royalist war leaders were not punished.

THE ARMY REMONSTRANCE

Charles had shown himself to be completely untrustworthy, constantly trying to play one side against the other. The New Model Army was already unhappy with Parliament, after its attempts to disband it. In November 1648, on behalf of the New Model Army, Henry Ireton now demanded that Charles be put on trial for being an enemy of his people. This was called the Army Remonstrance. But some MPs continued to negotiate with Charles. However, it was only after Parliament agreed to allow Charles to return to London that the army united against Parliament.

PRIDE'S PURGE

The army marched into London in December 1648. On 6 December, Colonel Thomas Pride prevented MPs who still favoured the king and who had signed the Treaty of Newport from entering Parliament. Some MPs were even arrested. This was known as Pride's Purge and the Rump Parliament was all that was left. It was made up of just 80 men and it was they who put the king on trial for treason.

During Pride's Purge, MPs who supported the King were arrested and banned from Parliament.

THE RUMP ACTS

The Rump announced that, "The people are, under God, the original of all just power", so they argued this meant that they had "supreme power in this nation". They were saying that they didn't need a king to govern the country. They set up a High Court of Justice to try Charles. There was a struggle to find someone willing to judge a king – the Lord Chief Justice of England refused – but eventually John Bradshaw, an anti-Royalist judge, agreed to put King Charles on trial.

CHAPTER 5

CHARLES ON TRIAL

Charles's trial took place at Westminster Hall from 20 January 1649. The High Court of Justice had 135 members but not all attended the trial. Sir Thomas Fairfax and Oliver St John were among those who did not go to Westminster Hall. Security was very tight at the trial: soldiers were brought in to control the crowds, cellars were searched and guards patrolled the roof. Judge John Bradshaw feared assassination from a possible rescue attempt for the king, so he wore a bulletproof helmet during the trial.

Parliament had the problem of what to charge the king with – since the 14th century, treason by definition meant the crime of attempting to overthrow or kill a monarch. Charles could not be accused of making war on himself. So Parliament invented a new definition of treason: "It is treason in the King of England... to levy [make] war against the Parliament and Kingdom of England".

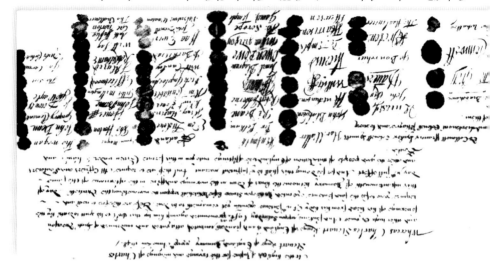

Only 57 members of the court signed King Charles I's death warrant, shown here. The 57 included Cromwell and Ireton.

Charles appeared before the judges four times, but he always said he did not believe in the authority of the court. Could the king be tried in a court of law or was he above it, having been appointed by God? The king was responsible for law, so Parliament could not legally create a court of justice. Charles refused to plead guilty or not guilty: "I cannot answer this till I be satisfied of the legality of it [the court]." As he pointed out, the whole of Parliament was not even there – the Lords were missing, as were the MPs who had been turned away during Pride's Purge.

Bradshaw refused the king permission to give a speech in his own defence and then presented the Parliamentary viewpoint. The king was found guilty on 27 January 1649. He was to be beheaded at Whitehall on 30 January 1649. He gave a speech saying that he wasn't the one who started the war.

AFTER THE KING'S DEATH

In March 1649, the Rump Parliament got rid of the House of Lords and the monarchy, saying it was "useless and dangerous". In May, they declared that England was a Commonwealth. A Council of State was set up to run the country, which consisted of 41 councillors, most of whom were MPs. John Bradshaw was the first president of the Council of State. They were to rule alongside the House of Commons.

In May 1649, Cromwell had to put down a revolt by the Levellers. They were a dangerous group who had been part of the New Model Army since 1647. It was these soldiers who rebelled.

THE LEVELLERS

The Levellers first appeared in southern England towards the end of the First Civil War. They represented ordinary working people, but were never a united group. *An Agreement of the People* was their idea for a new written constitution. They wanted more representation for the people in government and freedom to worship.

IRELAND

The Commonwealth was not secure until it dealt with its enemies close to home, so Cromwell headed to Ireland in August 1649, having become Lord Lieutenant of Ireland in June. Cromwell remembered the 1641 Rebellion, when 12,000 out of about 40,000 Protestants were killed in Ireland. He took 15,000 men and marched to Drogheda just north of Dublin. After a week of besieging the city, he asked them to surrender on 10 September. They refused, so he bombarded the city walls and thousands were massacred. This was in line with the rules of warfare at the time.

The massacre at Drogheda was unlike anything else in the Civil Wars, in which 2,000–4,000 people were killed during the siege of the town.

Cromwell became one of the most hated men in Ireland after the massacre, as it was he who had given the order of no quarter (no mercy). He hated Irish Catholics and wanted revenge for 1641. He also considered the massacre a warning to other Irish towns and cities.

The town of Wexford suffered a similar massacre a month later. Cromwell's aim had been to get Ireland under control as quickly as possible. He achieved his aim by May 1650, when he returned to England.

SCOTLAND

Charles I's son, also called Charles, had sailed to Scotland in June. Parliament became concerned that Charles and the Scots would invade England, so they sent Cromwell north to prevent the invasion. In July 1650, Cromwell arrived in Scotland with about 15,000 men. The Royalists had about 25,000, led by Alexander Leslie, Earl of Leven. At first, the fighting was kept to around Edinburgh, with the Scots preventing a full-scale battle from taking place. But when Cromwell moved to Dunbar, just south of Edinburgh, Leslie saw his chance and followed. Unlikely as it was, on 3 September, Cromwell defeated the Scottish Royalists at the Battle of Dunbar.

Cromwell had been unable to finish off the Royalists, so he did not prevent them invading England, believing that the English would join the fight against the invaders because they hated the Scots even more than the Rump Parliament did. At Scone, in January 1651, the Scots crowned Charles II king, and then they marched into England.

BATTLE OF WORCESTER

Charles continued on to Worcester, arriving on 22 August. Cromwell soon reached Worcester with 30,000 men – Charles had about a third of that number. The Battle of Worcester took place on 3 September. It would become the final battle of the English Civil War.

Charles showed great bravery during the battle, but as it dawned on most Royalists that they were going to lose, even their king could not inspire them any further. Reluctantly, Charles escaped the city in a desperate cavalry charge down the streets of Worcester and out of the city. The Parliamentarians then stormed the city from three directions, easily overwhelming the remaining Royalist troops and taking the city by nightfall.

Over 2,000 Royalists were dead and a further 10,000 Scots were captured and imprisoned. However, Cromwell reported to Parliament that the battle was "as stiff a contest as ever I have seen". The Royalist cause was finished, and the Parliamentarians had lost only 200 men.

CROMWELL IN CHARGE

romwell finally dismissed the Rump Parliament in April 1653. His hopes for Parliamentary reform came to nothing. Parliament also wanted to reduce the army's power. Much of what Cromwell did was based on his strong Puritan beliefs. So if he felt Parliament was not doing the right thing, he was happy to transfer allegiance to the army if he thought that would advance the religious cause. This made him very unpopular.

BAREBONES PARLIAMENT

The Barebones Parliament sat from July to December 1653. It included religious men chosen by Cromwell. Once again, however, Cromwell and the army decided to dissolve Parliament. The MPs were arguing among themselves and were talking about more radical reform than Cromwell thought the country would accept.

REFORMING THE NATION

Puritans became more powerful during the Protectorate, which led to changes in the churches – they were much plainer than before. Dancing, theatre and horse racing, among other things, were also banned.

Cromwell dissolved the Barebones Parliament in 1653. Most MPs chose to resign and the army forcibly removed the rest.

THE PROTECTORATE

In December 1653, Cromwell became Lord Protector. He ruled by the Instrument of Government, a set of laws drawn up mainly by army officers. Many were upset with the idea of the Protectorate. Cromwell was accused of planning it all along, abandoning his beliefs about religion and freedom. In October 1654, three army officers declared that the Instrument of Government gave Cromwell greater powers than the king had had. In fact, many people called him "Highness".

MAJOR-GENERALS

In spring 1655, there were a few attempts at Royalist risings. Cromwell had dissolved the first Protectorate Parliament, and he decided that military government was needed. England was divided into 12 areas, with a Major-General from the army in charge of each. Each Major-General reported directly to Cromwell and was able to raise militia, paid for by a tax on Royalist landowners.

CHAOS

Upon Cromwell's death in 1658, his son Richard became the new Protector. But he was not so able a leader as his father. Soon England was in chaos again. Spring 1659 saw Parliament and the army clash, and in May, the army restored the Rump Parliament. Richard retired and England was declared a Commonwealth once more. The Rump once again clashed with the army and was dismissed in October. There was no strong leader to run the country.

Cromwell soon realized that military rule was unpopular, so it was brought to an end in early 1657 with the Humble Petition and Advice. This new constitution suggested a return to a more traditional form of government. Cromwell was offered the throne, but he refused it. Instead, he was reinstated as Lord Protector in June 1657.

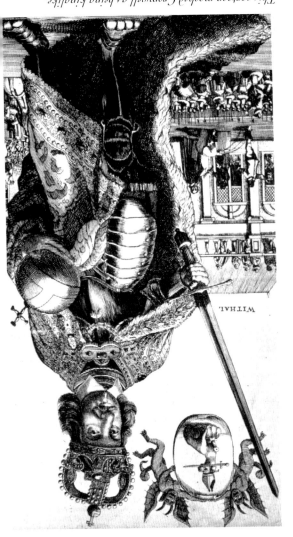

This cartoon mocked Cromwell as being kinglike.

THE RESTORATION

People had grown tired of the strict Puritans. Many felt that it might be good to have a king again.

General Monck, leader of the Scottish army, marched south to London. Nobody wanted another civil war, so when Monck entered London in February 1660, he took control. Members of the original Long Parliament were recalled, and they dissolved themselves after calling for free elections. The new Parliament decided that restoration of the monarchy would save England. Charles agreed to settle any issues that Parliament had had with his father, Charles I, so he was invited to return to England in May 1660 and become king.

A RETURN TO MONARCHY

The result of all the battles and bloodshed was a return to the type of government that had ruled England before, although Parliament made sure that its role was more powerful than it had been under Charles I. But overall, Charles I's death had changed little. Charles II was restored to the throne. Many people in England celebrated.

INDEX